THE SECRET HISTORY

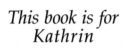
*This book is for
Kathrin*

Contents

Author's Note / 9

I
Caput Mortuum / 13

II
To my Father / 17
All Saints' Day in Konz / 43
White / 54
The Tunic of Christ / 56
Break of Day on Patmos / 59
Il ritorno in patria / 63

III
Home Coming / 67
The Kid / 69
From Fatehpur Sikri / 71
Zé Peixe / 73
The Shadow of Death / 74
Television / 78
Winterreise / 79

IV
Photographs of K. / 87
Industry / 91
New York, New York / 93
Kiss / Bliss / 95
Golbach / 97
The Wind at Vinci / 99
The Secret History / 101
The Garden / 103

V
To our Unborn Daughter / 109

Biographical Note / 113

Author's Note

This book has been a long time in the making. As I began writing the poems for my then partner Dorle in the early Nineties, and other poems in conversation with my father after his death in April 1994, it became clear to me that fundamentals of my own life were being addressed; and, as a body of poems started to come together, my subject defined itself as the quest for home. In my own case, finding a sense of being at home in my own life has involved coming to terms with the difficult legacies of the two nations, England and Germany, that were given to me at birth, and trying to decide which I could identify with, if either. For many years, living in Germany, I would say if asked that I felt at home in Germany but in the English language, and essentially that feeling remains true to this day. Finding a home has also meant seeking ease of spirit in a life without God, and rejecting an understanding of the world predicated on power politics. It seemed to me important to get the poems I wrote on these matters "right", to my own satisfaction, because I expected (and expect) to write only one book of an essentially autobiographical nature, and because I owed it to the others, particularly my parents, whose lives I was exploring in the poems. To write with no sense of hurry, and little concern for the marketplace, came to seem extremely important if I was to get anywhere near the "truth" of my sense of home.

I owe particular thanks to Keith Botsford, Greg Gatenby, Peter Goldsworthy, Robert Gray, Frank Kearful, John Kinsella, and the late Saul Bellow and Alan Ross, for timely critical support during the long gestation of this book. For a quiet place to write, thanks to George Ellenbogen and Evelyn Shakir for their cottage on Cape Cod, and to Marita Merkel for her house in the Eifel.

I

Caput Mortuum

An apple orchard, meadows and a river,
a raft at a mooring where children are swimming,
an ancient ash, the sawmill and the bridge,
and at the heart the home of all our colours –

tin pales of white lead paste, and silver mica
from China, and zinc oxide from Peru,
Carrara dust, pozzuoli, burnt sienna,
red ochre, aniline, Verona green,

dammar resin, madder lake, campeachy,
bone black, indigo and dragon's blood,
Dutch pink and gallnuts, dried black mallow flowers,
kamala, berberis root and walnut shells,

and dark in the stillness a man with a mortar and pestle,
cracking the lapis lazuli apart,
grinding the purest in the pulverisette,
a second grinding, then a sifting,

binding the powder with turpentine resin
and heated beeswax, letting it draw for a day,
then straining it in a linen bag
in a bucket of lukewarm water,

colour coming in a tide,
filling fifty pales, returning
to the first to pour the water off
and dry the sediment and sift again –

this, I think as I gaze beyond the river where the children swim,
beyond to where the sky consoles
with old familiar colours of our physics and our souls,
this in our stillness is our purest blue.

II

To my Father

Salt & Son have goldfish in a tank,
a box of tissues placed for customers,
the saviour on his cross, and photographs
of older Salts and hearses drawn by horse.

I made my way out back, through stacks of coffins,
looking for the room they call the chapel.
Someone unseen was whistling at his work,
someone else lay zippered on a trestle.

How did you get in here? he asked, embarrassed,
a beef-complexioned foxy youth
with bottlebrush hair and a ring in one ear.
I've come to see my father. William Hulse.

So this is it. The chapel. What a place.
Plastic flowers. A cross. Consoling light.
Two straight-backed chairs. The coffin lid
stood upright in the corner.

That charcoal suit was never really you,
and after all the weight you lost of late
you seem so little in it. Like a boy
in granddad's clothes. There's nothing left of you.

You're not yourself. Your face is solemn, waxy,
gone angular. Your glasses fit all wrong.
You smell of something strange. You're cold and hard:
I touch you, and you're terrible to touch,

and on my neck the hairs rise up in ice,
stiff with death, like when I was a boy
and you read 'Danny Deever' to me. And
his soul passed overhead.

II

Did I ever tell you about that song of Grieg's
that Mrs. Sterling taught us one Tuesday,
a classful of snotty Potteries kids,
in music at junior school in Chell?

An old man was singing of the spring he knew
would be his last: the greening of the grass,
the blossoms and the birdsong and the streams.
I was in tears and couldn't sing a note.

This April, since the last time I saw you alive,
the song's been repeating in my head
for another old man who would soon be dead,
whose going was the greater for the knowing:

Dad, you knew
this April was your last. I knew it too.
I held you shaking with the knowledge
when I sat you up in bed,

coughing and gagging, the eyes staring out of your head
with effort and fear of death.
I knew what you knew
as I held you, frightened and fighting for breath.

III

You'd understand this: when I knew you were dead,
I wept to think that I wouldn't be able
to shave you again. Not much of a service, perhaps.
But still, I longed to render it once more.

You'd lie with a towel gathered at your neck,
I'd lather you and draw the slackened flesh
tight for the blade,
and always you'd murmur *Sweeney Todd*

and giggle quietly in that way you had,
boyish and helpless, in the last month or so
when even laughing called for more strength than you'd left,
and I'd shave you with a plastic disposable razor,

and as often as not, since talking was hard,
I'd find myself thinking about the men
whose dying left a scar upon your mind:
Socrates, Seneca, Rommel.

I'd try to look them in the eye.
I'd try to know the men they were,
leading the life of action or the life of contemplation,
strongest of heart in the leaving it:

the soldier telling his wife to expect a call
from the hospital, and the usual telegrams,
and climbing into the car with General Burgdorf,
who held the poison ready in his fist,

the gadfly draining the cup at a draught,
walking among his friends till his legs were numb,
then waiting calmly for the final cold
to come with its tranquillity and healing,

and Nero's man – how old can I have been,
fifteen or so, when first I heard you say
that rather than await the worse to come
you'd opt for Seneca's way?

You scared me shitless at the time.
I hadn't realised your god
might just as well be noble, cruel, petty or sublime,
the milk of human kindness or a murderous old sod –

you'd no idea. None. And I can't shave you any more.
It's in my fingers still, the touch I needed,
that rhythm that was practice born of love.
But death has dulled my fingers like a glove.

IV

Your ash stick in the hall. Your pension book.
Your slippers, missal, cardigan,
the coronation spoon we fed you with.
Where shall I look for you now? –

on the black harbour water,
taking the bodies
of Japanese shot
in Stanley Prison

out in the night, beyond
the Hong Kong three-mile limit,
wrapping them in army blankets,
weighting them with bricks? –

or writing this letter from Singapore,
businessman to friend and Member,
wanting him to go to work
to save a Pahang Communist from hanging,

stapling a clipping to the carbon
afterwards: *Girl bandit Wong
Ah Lan, 18, won't hang.*
– I visited the temple on Penang,

that dark narcotic mystery you loved,
where at the start of every rainy season
pit vipers by the score
seek shelter and are welcomed in,

and when my eyes adjusted to the gloom
I made them out on wicker cribs and cradles,
lethal, lovely, lazy with joss and eggs,
ignorant of death. – Shall I look for you

in 626 Water Transport Company,
Lee Enfield number 25648,
waiting for Zipper, sure you'll be the first
to get your head blown off on a landing craft,

or shall I go back further, to a boy
as bright-eyed and original as Abel,
the boy who rejoiced, not an hour before he died,
in this bunch of April forget-me-nots on the table?

v

She was the shadow I think I see,
grazing her Chinese lips
on your cheek as the rocking Dakota
touched the tarmac in Bangkok,

the shadow in the dark
driving the Vanguard, one hand off the wheel,
her smile at sixty in the Malacca night
overturning you,

the shadow love
who went into the world of light
taking and leaving a photograph
of you at Kek Lok Si

that caught you
like a shutter
half a lifetime later:
ah, the Chinese girl.

Your drunken boss Caerlion had done a bunk,
leaving you to run the show
for R. J. Wood & Co.,
offices on Raffles Place above the Chartered Bank,

Lancashire textiles, end of empire, thinning order books –
Dad, for your past I wish you frangipani nights,
a Chinese melody brimful as love in your throat,
a touch, a look, a flutter in the heart –

the shadow I think I see.
For then you were the man without a shadow,
the company bankrupt, Asia at your back,
disembarking in a trenchcoat and a homburg at Marseilles.

VI

And then you took yourself a German wife
and headed home and settled near to Mother –
Mother who remembered Mafeking relieved,
churchbells ringing the length and breadth of England,

Mother who had views on Roger Casement,
Mother who knew her Shakespeare and the Bible back to front,
Mother who meant New Zealand lamb, a flutter on the National,
Jersey potatoes, ships at Liverpool, home-made damson jam,

and every April daffodils on Wordsworth's grave at Grasmere.
– When is a man a man? It was war,
between the woman you loved as a wife
and the woman who'd given you life.

In photographs I see her young,
wearing shapeless Twenties dresses,
long-jawed as Virginia Woolf,
proper as Queen Mary,

thirty-odd, with her Bubbles son
in Burslem park among the ducks,
the boy who'd one day volunteer
to fight for the stone in the silver sea. For England. And for her.

I have it on my shelf here as I write, her Mephistopheles,
Doulton, Machiavellian ware, a two-faced piece of work,
one side all grinning bonhomie, the other doom and woe.
I keep it as she had it on her mantel,

the smiling, cheerful side to the world –
the other face, the grief she wore
at the thought of the German bride her boy had married,
mourning its Staffordshire misery to the wall.

VII

After a boyhood of thinking you knew the answers,
I've kept a taste for trying questions on you.
For instance, climbing the terraces
of Sans Souci, Frederick's palace at Potsdam –

if you'd been there, I imagine I might have said,
This man they called the Great, who liked his wars and flute,
had a vineyard planted right here on this slope –
when was it re-planted with these figs?

You might have known. Or might have said, *I wonder,*
implying by your kind, inquiring tone
that knowing that we do not know is neighbour to the knowing.
Or idle speculation would have kept us occupied:

perhaps the vines were removed by a latter-day Kaiser?
Or else by the Communist ideologues
of the Democratic Republic, with their hatred of anything Prussian.
And maybe we'd have talked of Micah's time

when every man shall sit under his vine
and under his fig tree, and none shall make them afraid.
Anything rather than talk of the labour of marriage,
that long and steady toil that left the honeymoon of hope

and happiness imprisoned in the past,
slowly becoming historical, slowly fading,
fading like the photograph that showed your bright-eyed bride,
her dress spread round her like a parachute,

in the garden of that farmhouse near Hawkshead
where you'd spent endless carefree hours of childhood,
where Beatrix Potter walked across from Sawrey for the rent,
sturdy, dour and English in her coat,

and where the waterwords of the stream beyond the drystone wall
were always *sans souci*, and *sans souci* again,
and *sans souci* for all of the future
and *sans souci* for all of the past

as your newly-wed wife climbed the treadworn stairs,
threw wide the window, and took a deep breath:
bracken, beeches, earth, and rain hung close on the hill,
a smell as English as Esthwaite, a weather of Jeremy Fisher.

VIII

Blown off the Wall by Easter wind and rain,
we're sheltering in the lee of a lonely farm,
no other sign of comfort or of warmth
in all Northumberland, for all I know,

and you, with your nose in your precious book,
ferreting out a passage again
in your tattered vade mecum,
the indispensable Collingwood Bruce,

you tell me that a hundred years ago
the chives once planted by the legion
stationed here at Walltown
were growing in the grasses still, sixteen centuries on.

God knows I'm used to hearing things like this.
My childhood has been spent in other ages,
a game of hide-and-seek in ancient ruins.
My family includes the Roman Empire.

And so I'm unsurprised by what comes next.
Chives, you announce, *are indestructible.*
If they were here a century ago,
they'll be here still. We only have to look.

Of course I look at the field and think you're mad.
I'm soaked and cold and all I see is grass.
But no — you're a boy. A husband, father, man – but still a boy.
Like me, your son. We are two boys together.

And when at last, exulting, and unchastened by the weather,
we find the chives in the wild wet grass, and in my quickened mind
I see the Iberian legionnaire
who planted herbs of home away from home,

the world has undergone a change –
to live in time is to grasp the hand
of a man at his work in a kitchen garden,
a man long dead but no more dead than you are, Dad, today.

IX

Whatever became of Julie Babbington?
If ever I think of her, she's on the settee
that time I surprised you, skirt around her waist,
sweet sixteen, unflustered, a flush in her cheeks.

One afternoon when I came home from school,
Mum was beside herself and a woman was leaving,
righteous, mousy. Mrs. Babbington.
She'd found a letter in her daughter's bag.

For heaven's sake –
a clever, leggy schoolgirl who wore minis small as tissues,
and Mum forever failing at her diets.
Something in the way she moves

attracts me like no other lover.
When I thought of how often you'd asked me to play that song,
I froze. Had it occurred to Mum?
I thought of her temper and stopped playing *Abbey Road*.

She sent you back to Mother for the winter.
Nine months apart. The walking in parks. The talking.
She wanted your watch back, which had been her father's.
I still hear your snivelling whimper: *Heidi, my watch.*

Nine months. All smiles and making up one minute,
the next the knives were out again.
You brought out the worst in each other:
cowardly, cruel, wreckers in spite of yourselves.

One day, when I'd taken Mum's part in a quarrel,
we stood by the coal bunker, back of the house,
and you gave me one of your looks and told me
I hadn't the guts of a louse.

You see, I've not forgotten.
You don't forget if your father says something like that.
And yet, it seems so proper, now the pain is past,
to think of you so cruel in your panic:

of all you ever taught me, Dad, this means the most –
that nothing human should be strange to me.
I think of that letter you wrote to your parents-in-law,
in quavery German, when I was born,

full of the thrill of fatherhood,
wings at the heels of every word,
and I think of that other letter, the note
you wrote to Mum in hospital, after a difficult birth,

telling your Catholic wife you hoped your son
would be spared the Catholic darkness:
she wept again years later when she showed
that letter to me, during your winter apart,

and others you'd written from Asia, telling
of Bangkok's wats and klongs, Penang, Darjeeling,
horse-riding in the Himalayas,
readings in Marcus Aurelius and Plato,

the pleasures of an honest heart
gone rotten now (she told me, retying the ribbon,
stuffing the bundle of letters back into the drawer
and slamming the drawer shut) – rotten, dishonest and dark.

X

I could have stared forever at the fence-post and the blossom.
They seemed to be telling me how she died –
how, round a long slow bend in a country road,
a stranger's hurry stove in the side of her life.

Only a day or so ago it happened, as it does:
my foot slipped on the clutch, the car was stalled,
skewed across the camber of a lane,
dead in a three-point turn. Like Mum that day.

What were the last things she saw? –
the laundered white of the hawflower? or the wood-knots in a post?
a snag of grubby wool on a barb of wire?
the thousand familiar faces of God in a cloud?

That afternoon when the call came through
I'd been in the bath for a couple of hours,
topping the hot water up with a toe,
sipping self-pity and gin and reading Chandler.

There's been an accident. I stood there dripping,
a towel round me though I was alone
and no one sees you're naked on the phone.
Your father's in hospital. But he'll be all right.

You didn't drive. *And what about my mother?*
He didn't want to say, the ambulance driver,
having to hurt where care would have him help.
If you don't mind, I'd rather not say on the phone.

You'd been thrown clear. In hospital I found you in a daze,
too much the stoic to lose your mind, uncomprehending, conscious.
No more of her fads, her songs, her rages. No more out-of-body stories.
No more rolling naked in hay to stave off rheumatism. No more love.

The kindness of strangers. The constable and sergeant
lamenting nineteen to the dozen about the striking miners –
although their grief was real, to think that workmates
killed each other with blocks of concrete pushed off motorway
                                                    bridges,

it seemed they talked to occupy my mind.
I signed for the effects left in the car.
Against the tears, I opened her umbrella
and showered crumbs of glass from the shattered windscreen.

For you, ten years of loneliness. And always in that time
I would be flung right back to one of my earliest memories,
you hallooing across a river for the ferryman,
rain setting in, the suitcases steadily darkening as they soaked.

Christ says that in the resurrection
there is neither man nor wife;
but when did words have power to stay
the bone-old longing for a life

in which there'll be no parting any more?
I've kept it to this day, that paragraph
you clipped a year or so before you died
and sent me without comment:

The only black-browed albatross known in British waters
is back on Unst in the Shetland Islands where,
nearly every spring since 1972,
it has waited in vain for a mate.

XII

Pausing in your Gibbon at the passages you marked –
the noble spirit of Aurelius,
the salutary balm of Boethius,
the fortitude of Julian –

I see you reading in a pool of light,
a studious young man in Singapore,
with six good volumes named for Everyman;
so shortly after Belsen and Treblinka

restoring, by the scruple of the act,
the faith that words can say what living means,
can name the spirit in our brief machines –
calm and intrepid in the barbarian night.

We walked at Brothers Water
when your words were mostly blotted by a stroke,
and hazarded at what on earth you meant,
more than a pantomime but past a joke,

parading an imaginary cross –
a priest? – till in the end,
associating Marlowe's lines,
we got the word you wanted: caterpillar.

All winter long your own decline and fall.
Till all the words of all the histories
had come, on a certificate, to these:
Bronchopneumonia. Cerebrovascular disease.

XIII

What would I give to stand with you again
before that boar that thundered across a clearing towards us once,
standing as high at the shoulder as the shoulder of a man,
making our stunned bones jump and thud with every running
                                               thump.

What would I give to hear you tell again
(your table-talk) of red-hot irons up King Edward's anus
or William's bloated body, like a blown-up football bladder,
pricked and deflated to fit it in its coffin.

What would I give to see you laugh again
at Stan and Ollie malarking their lives away
or another repeat of another repeat of *Only Fools and Horses*,
half knowing, half remembering that what you saw was funny.

What would I give to know you in your bed,
your reassuring breathing rising steady, falling, rising,
a tide-line soughing in the Babylisten at my side:
in, out, in, out, in, out, in…

– Instead I'm reading what the nurse from Allied Medicare recorded:
"Bill was very tired today. He managed ½ a glass of water,
½ a glass of Build-up. Bill has had a bowel motion.
He has not eaten any lunch. He is not feeling well."

40

XIV

Come to thy journey's end with a good grace,
the stoic wrote, *just as an olive falls*
when it is ripe, praising the earth that bare it,
grateful to the tree that gave it growth.

Dad, I'm afraid you'd approve of this churlish priest,
saying the requiem for his friend deceased,
damning as pagan the passage we asked him to read,
dismissing as hopeless the Roman's natural creed,

his human love of this life, not the next,
preferring Newman, as he must,
and preaching his afterlifing text
over your coffin'd dust.

You know I feel he treads you in the dirt.
The anger chokes me. Dad, he does you hurt.
Your lifelong friends Aurelius and Christ
gave equal measure to your mortal heart.

What does he know of hope, what has he known,
who tells us there is hope in Christ alone?
What does he know of hope, who will not see
the wisdom of the olive and the tree?

And yet: he was your Father. And your friend.
And in my heart I know you'd say he's right
to guide us to the way, the truth, the life.
So, Dad, for your sake, at your journey's end,

I'll kneel to him, and to your god, today.
But, where no priest can hear, to you I say:
I shall not look upon your like again.
To that, amen.

William Ernest Hulse, 1925-1994

All Saints' Day in Konz

I

At the foot of the concrete campanile
of the post-war church like a paper hat
we stop to shelter from the rain, my cousin Adelheid and I,
and gaze at the muscled confluence
that gave this German town its Latin name,
the remnant few vermilion bricks
of Valentinian's winter residence,
and a churchyard full of kith and kin

where this first day of Catholic November
mantled candles burn on graves
and the priest, umbrella held for him
by a cassocked boy in Reebok running shoes,
dispenses blessings on the dead,
progressing like a pope
among the families and the sole survivors,
the faithful all in black or grey (my cousin is in pink).

In this good earth my mother's mother lies,
who recalled with a tickle of trivial guilt
that time she climbed over the orchard wall
of the Trier cathedral chapter
to pilfer her fill of their cherries – *A hatful!* she chuckled,
prim in her pinafore on a kitchen chair
like poor Mrs. Tittlemouse wearied by her work,
twinkling at the aftertaste of sin.

Apart from her annals-of-history day,
that day of the Great Calamity, when
she put down her troublesome teeth on the table
then wrapped them in newspaper with the potato
peelings and bundled the lot in the stove,
I think she was always happiest at the range,
a touch-me-not air of absorption about her,
a that's-how-to-do-it, a bustle, a calm –

bowed to her kitchen devotions I see her,
greasing the griddle for waffles, preparing
the cutlets of pork (salt them and pepper them,
breadcrumb and brown, then fill up the pan
with water to cover, add cloves and a bay leaf,
and simmer an hour and a half –
an old Silesian recipe locked in her bones,
encoded as a prized ancestral secret).

The kitchen was sweetness and light. But religion
was darkness, mystery, cognac, cigars,
shut up in a cupboard for priests who called by
for a closeted hour of soul-talk that no one
(most certainly not a mere husband) was ever
allowed to intrude on. Till death she stuck out
an obstinate old-fashioned tongue for the host at communion,
refusing to take the body of Christ in her hand.

The plastic Virgin with her plastic Bernadette,
a souvenir of Lourdes, in pink and white and blue,
played a Sunday jingle if you wound her up.
And every Good Friday my grandmother retired
into the Bedroom of Christ of the Sacred Heart,
drew down the blinds against the dolorosa day,
and lay in the place of congress and of peace,
happy to suffer with her bloody god.

II

My mother is buried here as well. At least, her ashes are;
I carried the urn from England in a hold-all,
and left my mother in a luggage locker
to picnic in St. James's Park with Vicki.
– It puzzled me when I was small. *Heidi*.
How could there be a book about my mother?
But photos of her as a girl appeared to fit the bill.
That blonde idyllic smile. That air of dairy-farming freshness.

A childhood hijacked by Hitler and God…
the bull-blooded hot-collared head of the house
and her autocrat mother, implacable Catholic,
drumming her off to walk in white at every Corpus Christi
with a plaited *Heimat* innocence that suited the Almighty
and an Aryan girliness fit for the BDM –
while all along the vineyards, on the hills above the river,
the Siegfried Line was prophesying war.

By spring of 1945 the village was in ruins.
The occupying French were everywhere,
mamselling after anything in a skirt.
She was coming up to sweet sixteen. And up for air –
those years of Saint-Exupéry, Pearl Buck and Hemingway!
A teenager in the typing pool, twitchy with dreams of Paris,
wanting to be Grace Kelly, scraping the pfennigs
for nylons or a visit to Lake Constance.

Is it really true, as a friend observes,
that women are always disappointed?
That Englishman she'd been writing to
in Singapore, a universe away,
arrived with an air of the world one winter's day
and put up at the best hotel in town.
It must have seemed what she was waiting for.
A wedding day was fixed for June.

And then the move that changed it all:
from the rivers and forests she loved, a home
where the earliest vines were planted out by Romans,
he took her to start a life in Stoke on Trent.
A bike, a wife, a semi and a job
with the British Aluminium Company:
that, it appeared (and it terrified her), was the sum of his ambition.
Where was the brio she longed for? Where the passion?

Where the vision?

His mother had seen two German wars and didn't care for her.
The shopkeepers and bus conductors pretended
they didn't understand a word she said.
It was a war. And everyone was on the other side,
even her child: expert in English victory,
I won every dogfight astraddle a dining-chair,
machine-gunning Jerry out of the air:
ya-a-a-rmmm, uh-uh-uh-uh-uh-uh-uh-uh-uh.

– Identify the body. Jesus, I could hardly look.
Her face had twisted to a clench,
her jaw wrought sideways in a foxy wrench.
That one dropped lid that troubled her was terrible to see.
The sergeant coughed. Uneasily, I thought.
Your mother, he had said, *died instantly.*
She didn't feel a thing. And now I knew
that when I left the morgue I'd say the same.

But those last dying moments in the crash,
I've played them over till the needle's glowed:
birdsong perhaps, a creak of metal, a snatch
of yet another argument with Dad,
and then the smash of silence, like the day
in the garden when she put her foot
through his Chinese 78s –
the jealous crack of shellac, a long night without music.

III

This earth received my mother's father too.
When I remember him raising his glass
of star-and-crescent Turkish wine to the light,
I remember as well that he was in the Party.
When I remember him sucking his breakfast egg
with a lippy slurp that flipped my stomach over
and dabbing the glistening corners of his mouth with a damask
                                                    napkin,
I remember as well that he was in the Party.

He'd shave with a cut-throat razor and a badger-bristle brush
and a cake of soap, a jug of hot water, and a jug of cold,
at the kitchen table, taking twenty minutes:
it was like being in church. And many a time
he walked me by the railway, in the woods,
along the vineyards or the riverbank.
I remember as well that he was in the Party.
I remember as well that he was in the Party.

How often, in the forest, did he grip me by the hand,
silence me with an eyebrow and a hissing of the breath,
and whisper that the witch could not be far? –
listening for a snapping twig, a rustle in the trees.
– He had a wife. Two daughters. And a job.
A job on the council. Not to join meant Dachau.
I see the manchild unheroic sorrow in his heart.
I see a man so very like myself.

It is time for me now to think back, to think
of this man whom I knew at the end of his life,
wearied, weakened by illness, worn
to a ravelling solitude on a kitchen chair.
In thought I walk three thousand miles with him
from an Astrakhan p.o.w. camp, after Brest-Litovsk,
drinking the evening wine in the village squares
of Anatolia, every day closer to home.

Home? – The farm wouldn't go to the youngest brother,
so Josef had to make himself a life.
He found a job, and then he asked the girl
he'd talked to with the milk pail if she'd care to be his wife.
Gut Social Democrat, God-fearing husband, dutiful plodding
believer,
lacking for languages, money, alternatives, drive, imagination,
where should he go when the mayor took him gently aside
and explained unmistakably why he should join the Party?

Where? With what means? And how should I judge?
Or claim I'd have had the courage to resist,
I who have never been tested? The latter-day righteous
are certain that they would have done the heroic thing.
They flatter themselves they'd have taken a stand
(much as every last Frenchman was in the Resistance).
I say only this: I cannot judge the man.
I cannot, as long as I fear I'd have done the same.

IV

In childhood this was my summer home from home.
Apples and blackberries and plums
fattened in August heat. The harvesters
worked the fields. On every walk there were springs
to drink the cold clear water from, and shrines
to gather wildflowers for. I played
in ruined pill-boxes, tried to catch lizards
on vineyard walls, rode back on scarlet tractors.

The sprawling kitchen was steamy with cooking and rows,
the loud air crowded with squabbling hothouse love.
When they were eating and into their stride, the women
shared out their relish for death. A forefather on the railways
shunted between the buffers at St. Wendel, on the Saar
(this was in eighteen-fifty-something, but told as if it was yesterday).
Two lads from neighbouring Karthaus
drowned when a treacherous eddy caught their canoe.

And, as they talked, the dangers edged in closer to the table.
Relatives dead of cancer. A priest, a good friend of the family,
crushed when the tractor he'd hitched a ride on
overturned on a slope. And of course the bombing.
After one raid, my mother's sister Klara
emerged from a church after morning prayer,
got fifty yards, then froze as the house of God
came tumbling down behind her and lay dead in a heap of rubble.

51

The rain is easing off. The priest is done.
Time for a prayer, or something like a prayer, before we go;
for this is the day of the saints, and I come to this grave
to say my goodbyes once again to the home I once had.
My father lies here now as well, beside the wife he loved,
and so this corner of a "German" field
is just a little "English", I suppose. As if it mattered.
As if a patch of ground could have a passport.

A home is not given. It has to be made.
And often I think I've been straying all my life,
a baffled frightened boy without a clue,
amid the dust and debris of an Empire and a Reich,
when the Jacks have all been hauled down in the sunset
and the jackboots left outside the doors
in the Thousand Year Hotel.
At times I'd call it History. At times it feels like Hell.

If all the Empire had a single playing-fields-of-Eton face,
I'd slap it for its predatory, witless arrogance,
then sit it at a mirror till
it recognised the features of disgrace.
If I'd been there when the guards abandoned the camps,
if I had entered Birkenau or Belsen
and seen and touched the near-dead and the dead,
I'd have unbuilt the whole of Germany, stone by reeking stone.

I'd have been right. But I'd have been far more wrong.
A home is made in knowledge and forgiveness,
and these good dead were more than History,
they were my own dear flesh and blood,
they laughed and wept, they loved their wine and cherries,
and if I pray today it must be this:
whatever of the past I should inherit,
I'll want to choose a way to live that tallies with their spirit –

for when my thoughts turn inward to the home we love and lose,
one memory infallibly comes back:
I'm three years old and standing with my mother and my father
on the left bank of the Mosel, not so very far from here,
waiting in heavy rain for the ferryman…
and over in the downpour, somewhere almost out of sight,
the arches of a bridge destroyed in bombing in the war
stride like a heron into the flow, and stop halfway across.

Adelheid Elisabeth Theresia Hulse née Gebhard, 1928-1984
Josef Gebhard, 1895-1967
Dorothea Gebhard née Fabian, 1896-1987

White

Contentment dwelt under the pear tree where
he'd sit in the shade on a kitchen chair
    in shirtsleeves and braces,
his back to the beans and the dahlias,

hands like motoring gloves on his breast,
a cotton handkerchief draped on his face
    to show he was resting.
His handkerchiefs were a faded white, like

old snow or sloeflower, smelling of snowmelt,
of maleness and trouser pocket. He'd sit
    in the garden, listen
to chickens, bees, a neighbour's radio,

and close his eyes. And be in Astrakhan.
The prison camp. The hospital. The sky
    as bold and white as an
enamel bowl. As functional and bare.

I remember one day in the forest
we stopped at an anthill. *Don't poke at it*
    he told me quietly.
We stood there in the resin-scented shade,

watching the ants in the pine-needle hill
built high as my chest, working, unresting.
    He took the handkerchief
from his pocket, flapped it open, and placed

it carefully on the hill. *Now watch*. I watched.
He waited till the cloth was black with ants,
    then shook it clear. *Now put*
your nose to it. And instantly my head

filled with the formic acid reek of fear,
the thing he wanted me to understand:
    a white-out in the mind,
white as the heavens over Astrakhan,

white as the cool of an afternoon hour
in a sunshot garden under a pear
    tree, all of contentment
dwelling in the tent of a square of cloth.

Josef Gebhard, 1895-1967

The Tunic of Christ
exhibited in the Cathedral of Trier, 1959 and 1996

To wait here, torn in heart and mind,
in a querulous line of religious trippers
in sneakers and T-shirts and jeans,
to take a second look at a garment
that may have clothed the flesh of Jesus Christ,
the flesh of God incarnate, the god
in whom I cannot, if I would, believe;
to stand here half a lifetime later

and recollect the funeral patience
of solemn Sunday dresses, suits and ties,
throbbing Latin murmurous as diesel,
waiting first in the hard bright square
and then in the candle-dark cathedral
to see the tunic he wore in his final hours,
for which the soldiery cast their lots;
to bide the high story as if it were true

is to be that wide-eyed credulous boy again
in the Fifties gloom of adult obsession and grief,
the Catholic half-light of guilt and devotion,
of fear and deception and majesty,
a four-year-old led by the hand of a mother
and taken in trust to the heart of the dark,
delivered to all of the terror of ages –
in the name of the Father, and of the Son, and of the Holy Ghost.

I stood here then at the close of the decade
of bobby-socks, Korea, Dien Bien Phu,
Eisenhower, shark-fin Cadillacs,
kidney-shaped occasional tables,
Algeria, Stalin's death, and polka-dot frocks.
Then as a child I knew nothing. Now I know less;
and I'm here, in a city as old as the bread and wine,
to look once again at the tunic of Jesus Christ.

A darksome stuff it is. Untouchable. Frail
as the binding of a book gone brittle with age,
fissured like ancient paper, falling apart
with time, and meaning, and seeking after meaning,
flaking death from death, like slate or like shale,
scaled like the ochre ages of the earth.
A soil once good, ploughed and furrowed, crumbling now. A dust
again becoming dust before my eyes.

Nothing it is. To nothing it returns.
It is all things on earth. It is the earth.
To look at it is to behold myself,
the semblance of my nothingness,
my field, once fertile, left to lie fallow.
The binding of my book falling to dust.
The text of my life fading from the page.
The page itself as if it had never been written.

To find a consolation here!
To think Christ gone, but present yet;
dead, but risen; nothing, but everything, and for ever.
I have been trying to pray, or trying to try,
such tenderness I feel for that good man
so cruelly, indifferently killed;
and still I cannot think him more (or less)
than one good man killed as the world kills men.

This is a scrappy old fact of cloth. And my past
whispers how good it would be to believe in it all,
to believe in it all and to be a child again
and wander for ever amid the murmur of bees
in summer meadows with wildflowers over my head.
God knows I've been trying. God knows I've been wanting to try.
But I've walked on, and clear of the line, and out
to the sunshot dusk of a world becoming dust.

Break of Day on Patmos

Last night

we sat on the waterfront, at Pirofani's,
with fish and bread and wine. The seller of sponges
  shut up his shop. The vendors wheeled away
  the racks of cards, unhooked the dresses hung
    from doorframes, stashed the hats.

Widows came home from their sundown walks to the graves,
the backgammon players under the tamarisk
  rolled the dice and clacked the counters, and girls
  tightened their honeyed thighs on the men who
    drove the Hondas. Was there

a moment we missed? When the oleander faded?
Hibiscus ceased to burn? The pomegranate dropped
  in the dark? And the last of daylight went
  from off the face of the bay? When did the
    last of the boats come home?

First I was struck by an old man who worked the bars,
touting pistachios and cashews from a basket,
  exhausted, hardly trying, wearing a
  T-shirt that read: *Whatever your fear is,*
    look it in the eye. Then

came the stooped-over woman with the megaphone.
She prowled the promenade growling Apocalypse,
   judgement, the seven last plagues, the brimstone
   lake of fire. The ancient sadistic dross.
      The waiter, with a tray

of Amstel beers, translated, tapped his forehead. Was
there ever any woman so alone? I watched
   her raise the megaphone: *And in those days*
   shall men seek death, and shall not find it – did
      she care if anyone

was listening? – *and shall desire to die.* Entire
unto herself. Unmeek. By proxy merciless.
   The enemy of peace. She prattled on,
   the more to fear the emptiness without –
      and death shall flee from them.

I thought: I've a bone to pick with the joyless shit
who wrote the pernicious trash of Revelation.
   Was ever any woman so alone?
   Done good and proper by John the Divine,
      she'd lost so much of life

she no longer knew what it was. She hated it.
No more, if she had her way, would the flowers appear
   on the earth, no more would the south wind blow
   upon the garden, pomegranates bud.
      As for the bride and groom,

put out the stars, pulp all the frivolous mags, burn
the little black dress of Chanel and the sonnets
    of Petrarch, shut down the clubs and the bars,
    and silence all the turtles in the land:
        their voice shall not be heard.

The woman lowered her megaphone, shuffled on,
and I think if our end had come right there and then
    she'd have slouched on with a told-you-so smile,
    mettled and righteous, to meet the Divine
        in the dark.

             This morning

I went out before it was day to watch the dawn
gathering, filling the jasmine flowers with white and
    fleshing the firm tomatoes on the vine,
    ripening figs and firing with presence
        the wisdom of the world.

Shall I inherit the wind? The foxes have holes,
the birds of the air have nests; and I have a home,
    I scarce know where. The men on their Hondas,
    the daughters of musick, they are at ease
        or broken asunder,

they bloom in the glory of bougainvillea –
the love of many waxes cold, and maybe they're
    broken with breach upon breach, broken in
    pieces with words, but they wouldn't have missed
        a minute. The neon

cross that shone blue in the night snapped off at the touch
of a switch, the paprikas fattened with red, and
    the first of the fishermen went down to
    the water. Let me always take thought, of
        proud looks and lying tongues,

hands that shed innocent blood, gods putting witless
rhetorical questions: whether the rain has a
    father, whether we gather grapes from thorns.
    Wisdom is everything that is the case:
        green pastures, still waters,

backgammon counters, fish and bread and wine, the white
returning to the jasmine flowers. I sat and watched
    a solitary fishing boat put out
    across the bay. To the open water.
        Into the light.

Il ritorno in patria
i.m. Max Sebald

Returning to the Ionian town of his birth,
Seferis found the windows of his childhood home were broken;
the iron door was rusted; the shutters of the upper storey rotted.
He was unable to find his initials
which he had carved on a wall when he was ten.
The wheel-well still drew water —
a tiny donkey turned it, and a mulberry gave shade —
but the old plane tree had died
that bustled with sparrows in the afternoons.
Of the ten windmills that bristled on the hills behind the harbour,
all that remained were a handful of ruins.

Smyrna, he wrote in his journal, had lost its shadow.
At Ephesus the cyclamen wore tones of the Ionian sky.
What was the harbour was sunken now, dry ground,
the mouth of the tomb of a once great city
and its dead surrounding plain –
this was the conductor of the souls
of the vanished harbours of Asia Minor.

For the moment, he wrote, there is consolation
in twilight on the slopes of Ionia,
the cyclamen, in which one may sense the tremors
of the great soul of Heraclitus.

III

Home Coming

Leaving the Oldsmobile tickticking under a
maple, the driver who writhed off her panties and
    wanted my hand up her thigh, up
  the stickshifting muscle, up into her

wetness, walks naked across an Ontario
field, down the catwalk of sex, as if flesh were the
    latest Versace creation. And
  she fucks as women do who're not well loved,

her devil fast at her back with a glass of sand,
minute by sifting minute – as if the body
    could find the frequency of time
  and shatter death as a voice shatters glass.

– Away from you, I'm any man alone. Zapping
channels after midnight in a hotel bedroom.
    Whisky from the mini-bar. And
  missing you. And then at times the movies

run, of women I've known, their beauties, bodies, all
their other country matters: wonderfully nude,
    they flash upon that inward eye
  that stiffens the resolve of solitude,

they bid me drink champagne from the cup of their sex,
they want me to come in their hair, come on their breasts,
    rub in my cream and lick it off,
  they limber to the window saddlesore

and stand with a snailtrack of jism on their legs
as if to say, *behold*. – Still, when I run the films
    it's loneliness that hits. I know
   the flesh alone's no more than a hotel.

This body that honours yours, that quickens and thrills
to yours, your coming and ebbing, has a knowledge
    pulling below, tidal and deep
   as travels in the undertow of home:

beautiful animal, lover, assuager, friend,
remember our room by the deepwater channel,
    our shuttered room on Zattere? –
   curtains lifting like veils on a shifting

of air and the wedding-white shipping cleaving the
deep as we cleaved to each other and whispered for
    joy of a deep-draught passage – love,
   the current of displacement in the depths.

The Kid

Remember seeing him interviewed on TV,
that boy who played opposite Chaplin in *The Kid*?
     Sixty years on, his eyes were dim.
     His meaty carbuncular beet of a nose

was pulsing with veins of imperial purple
that looked like the terrible rubbery bits in
     liver that made your stomach heave
     when you were a kid yourself. Remember? We

tried hard to see the child who had fathered the man,
the scamp in the film, that six-year-old dodger who
     wore his artful innocence tipped
     at a streetwise angle, like his cap. No good:

the child was gone. The boy we'd fallen in love with,
who made us agree we'd like one like him ourselves,
     no longer existed except
     on celluloid. And in our heads. I thought of

that day at the races in Kuching, the little
Filipino girl you couldn't take your eyes off –
     wide-awake, gamine, alive. A
     girl who could be your second self. Or atone

for your abortion? That, I suppose, must be what
it comes down to: a kid is the road not taken,
     the self that has another chance
     and gets it all right – but no one could really

conceive of that bleary pensioner on TV
as a man who'd got anything right. The shock was
    mortal: might we fail our own past?
      That kid who watched for the cop at a corner

with Chaplin, that nipper who promised a life of
vitality, humour and love, seemed terribly
    (simply by wearing his cap) a
      betrayal of all that might have been if the

film had unreeled in ideal perfection. And
suddenly, in the palace of silent movies,
    we saw the kids we'd been ourselves
      surviving in gestures – jerking, dated, quaint

They never speak to us, those kids. They scarcely seem
to know that we are what they have become. Always
    they're looking for someone else, and
      though they reach out they can never hold our hand.

From Fatehpur Sikri

Knowing full well,
in my fortieth year,
that I know nothing,
often I wonder

what is right and fitting
in the living,
when knowledge of the debt we owe the dead
begins to hurt.

A woman at Fatehpur Sikri,
wanting a child,
was tying a thread
behind the tomb

of Salim Chisti, Akbar's priest,
her husband standing by,
and as she rose and turned away
I caught her eye, and knowledge passed between us.

Akbar, they say, walked barefoot from Agra,
having no son and heir, to see the priest,
and when his promised son was born
he had this palace built, and on the gate

the lesson he had learnt inscribed:
The world is a bridge.
Pass over it, but do not build
a house upon it.

Sitting in the sandstone courtyard
where the light falls on the walls
like warmth upon a skin,
I know I love you. And I know

that that is all I know.
I'm walking barefoot. Let us go
to scatter petals,
rose and marigold,

on the silken counterpane
of Salim Chisti's tomb.
Let us honour the living and the dead.
Let us tie a thread.

1995

Zé Peixe

José Martins Ribeiro, known as the Fish Man

If ever I should think I understand
the marriage of true bodies and true minds,
remind me of the pilot of Aracaju,
poorest seaport in Brazil,

guiding the ocean-going shipping
out of the tricky estuary
of the Rio Sergipe
to open sea, and diving off the rail –

the man they call Zé Peixe,
crawling through the miles of swell and foam
from where he cannot have a home to where he has no home,
in his element.

1996

The Shadow of Death

I

So long you kept me stacked in the blue!
No wonder I began to feel my age,
killing year after year, one eye on you,
one on the fuel gauge.

The story was as old as love itself:
as if you'd put a glass down at a party,
you'd lost sight of the secret, lost the knack,
till all that was left was the grief of lack.

We'd wished the mercy of growing old together,
only to find (as the poet said) that
you can't hold up the weather. In the end
I thought I must be going round the bend.

You thought it must be you. Between the bouts
of apathy and *Star Trek* on the box
you'd pack up your troubles for another romp
in childhood's attic with your psychopomp.

You wouldn't talk about the loss to me,
as if to name it would increase the woe:
since knowledge is but sorrow's spy,
you didn't think it safe that I should know.

Perhaps we never had a chance. Perhaps there is no art
to mend a love. Perhaps we were wrong-footed from the start.
Perhaps perhaps perhaps. What use are words?
It broke my heart.

II

In the beginning was love. Love as Christ
in the house of Martha and Mary, love
as Schiele's fever of the flesh, and love
as Stefan Lochner's virgin of the roses.

And then, with funding fingered from the wallet at Time's back:
the Vatican of the spirit and the Hermitage of the heart,
the Alexandrian library of tenderness and care,
the V & A of loss and consolation –

the Museum of Love. We became each other's keepers.
Curators of our retrospectives. Our custodians.
A time came when I thought that I'd become
the man with the memories in Helen's story –

one day they'd take me away in a clinical shift
to do something terrible to my head with knives
and you'd be left to wonder if
you wanted me to come back out alive.

– How did it feel, my love, as you ran from the ward
where the very air was labouring for breath?
– My face is foul with weeping,
and on my eyelids is the shadow of death.

III

Ich bin der Welt abhanden gekommen

It was as if the world had put me down,
a book once loved but now no longer read,
and wandered off with something else in mind,
some other epic fiction in her head,

now and then wondering what had become of me,
perhaps one day to happen on me, like
the wife in that cartoon that tickled you,
discovering her husband down the back of the settee –

so that's where you've been all these years.
I stared at the night. Afraid of the dark. Afraid to sleep
because of the dreams, and because of the waking.
I was a heap of fears. A fool. A parcel of vain aching.

I was Moll Flanders leading away the horse
from the door of the inn as a matter of course
because stealing was what she did and it was there.
Waking, it seemed, was what I did. I breathed the pointless air.

1996

Television

after Sappho

Because I am alone tonight
Anne Parillaud, in a little black dress,
a shift of savage emptiness,
unwraps her present like a child –

she grasps the meaning of the thrill,
takes out the bodyguard and the boss
in a swift, efficient kill –
let the Pleiades be where they will.

Because I am alone tonight
the moon is careless of its light
and Anna Kournikova slams
the ball home in a breaking smash

and though she'll never win the match
frankly I couldn't care less –
the point of tennis is to watch
her body moving in a dress.

But still no other flesh or face
can take your television place
and I am hurting at the bone
because tonight I lie alone.

1997

Winterreise

I've been a stranger here from birth,
a journeyman on homeless earth,
an ancient out of time, a boy,
a saddened heart surprised by joy,
a lover in ideal vein
acquiring expertise in pain,
supposing love might still redeem
the unaccommodated dream –

a man of faith without a god.
I write this, Dorle, from Cape Cod.
The trees have fretted into leaf,
stating a natural belief.
The moonlit beauty of the lake
quickens the unforgotten ache.
Here, once again, I'm passing through.
And, once again, I'm missing you.

September I returned to find
you'd thought it through, and knew your mind,
and had to go. I'd feared you would.
It made no sense. I understood.
Since then I've loved you, hated, tried
to forget you, liked it not and died –
and now, like Luther, look at me
planting my little apple tree.

With lovers, gods, and history,
the trash of nationality,
the dross of time, we think the war
is won if we're in love or score
the pyrrhic victories of art
over the knowledge of the heart.
– Say, if my pain falls silent, who
will ever give me word of you?

We thought it out of ocean's reach,
our sand-love promised each to each –
hieroglyphics on the strand
which now I no more understand
than smoke unscrolling from the joss
writing its ideograms across
the void and vanishing: I swear
our love was smokescrip, writ in air.

II

This spring I visited the grave
of a good friend who always gave
you all the greatness of the heart
and soul that you require of art,
one who lives on in minds made better
both by her spirit and her letter,
and brought you from that Highgate plot
this April's first forget-me-not –

if only consolation grew
with such a pure and peaceful blue!
Philosophy is all awry:
it simply waits for us to die,
making the odd assuaging noise,
providing us with clever toys
to while away the interim
from void to voided Elohim.

Our cancered friends who died too young
are words for silent music, sung
to a pitiless measure of the spheres:
we keep the time and count the years,
praying the substance that survives
will lend us grace to shape our lives.
Andreas. Karin. Come to dust.
As we too must. As we too must.

What is the point of all we make?
It never palliates the ache.
Even the Bach they play on Cape
Classical's subtly shifted shape:
without you, he's become a bore,
B flat and A C B, no more,
and Monteverdi hurts to hear
without my music lover near.

I see you bending to the keys,
the mistress of the harmonies,
your hair a curtain on your cheek,
the bone so fine, the flesh so meek,
inheriting with every tone
the world you justly call your own,
the Passion and the Pentecost.
– That touch of fire it is I've lost.

III

On this first sea-grey day of June
I spent the affectionate afternoon
with Jeff and Julie by the water,
watching their wide-eyed son and daughter,
pained to an exquisite degree:
the kids you wished to have with me
are limbo'd, powerless to be born.
Aborted. Unbegot. Forlorn.

These thoughts are good for nothing. Rather
follow the comedy of a father
trying to fly the children's kite
in breezes that refuse to bite
and act as if I weren't unduly
troubled by the grace of Julie,
a tranquil beauty through and through,
so disconcertingly like you.

My days are like the aftermath
of war. – I thought I'd found the path
out of the wild unholy wood.
I thought that I was home for good.
For childish notions such as this
the gods keep an ancient nemesis,
and, when it hits, their age-old song
has a familiar chorus: *Wrong*.

Assuming I've three score and ten
to serve in all, like other men,
that leaves near thirty still to do –
so many years of missing you,
so many years of marking time
in this *monotonous sublime*,
of making sense where none is given.
My days are snowfall, blown and driven.

Three thousand miles away you sleep,
and that your dreams be safe and deep
and that you witness when you wake
a day but not a lifetime break
I write this *gute Nacht* in snow
to tell you what I know you know:
Dorle, my friend, my infidel,
I love you. And so fare you well.

    Cape Cod and Cologne, 1997

IV

Photographs of K.

.

1935, Lucien Aignier

Benito Mussolini
squeezes his offending nostrils
absolutely shut
with leather-gloved efficient fingers,
stifling a ticklish undignified threat of a sneeze,
and keeps his pig-at-the-abattoir eye
securely fixed
on the fawning Party faithful come to see him off at Stresa.

Unobserved on another platform,
called by no one to attention,
petulantly K. leafs through
a page or two
of a history of Abyssinia,
slipping her sandals off and rubbing a foot against her calf.

II

1939, Erwin Blumenfeld

High on the topmost girder of the Tower,
keeping a steely grip on a strut,
Lisa Fonssagrives
fans out for Paris *Vogue* the breezy calico swatch of a dress
that looks like a chequered café tablecloth,
swirling it out in a billow from her hand
as if inviting any idle wind
to parachute her into evermore.

Under a flowering almond tree
on the Seine embankment far below,
K. accepts a cigarette
from a man who's propped his bike against the railings,
a young photographer from Chanteloup,
who leans to brush a blossom from her hair.

III

1942, I. Russell Sorgi

To mourn a single unknown life among so many unknown dead
may seem perverse: but there she falls, this divorcee about to die,
outside the Genesee Hotel, in Buffalo, N.Y.,
falling, of her own volition, to the street below,
and the man at the coffee shop window, the man
whose attention has wandered from his *New York Times*,
may glimpse her as her body passes, or may hear a thud,
and may run out when others start to shout.

Elsewhere in a winter fastness
K. walks into a silent clearing,
January sunlight on her brow,
leaving a track in the snow
and bringing back the great and leafless wood
to green and goodly thought.

IV

1945, Dave Scherman

The silverware in this apartment's monogrammed A.H.,
signed copies of *Mein Kampf* are stood in stacks,
and in the bathroom a statuette
of a sturdily-waisted German maiden
with regulation breasts and hair
looks on in defeated disbelief
as Lee Miller leaves her combat boots on the mat
and soaps herself in Hitler's tub.

K. wears her naked truth to sleep
and when she's pillowed on a dream
the softer rise and fall of night
repairs the damage of the day
and offers promises to keep,
and flushes her, and tousles her, then wakes her woes away.

Industry

Not even you would call him industrious
who sits up for the sake of a girl

Epictetus

It's one thing to hold the body no more than
       an ass with a pack-saddle on –
       I can imagine letting go
when a soldier comes and lays hold of the beast;
       and all of the bridles and the shoes,
       the oats and hay, he's welcome to.
One day I'll be ready, I think. But what of now?

Bubbles rise to the air in her glass. She draws
       her feet up under her. She smiles,
       troubling my blood with her beauty,
and suffers the firelight to find an Order
       of Lenin, a silver crucifix,
       and the burnished flesh of her cheek.
Again I'm sitting up for the sake of a girl.

Desire and aversion are in your own power –
       why care about anything else?
       She tells me it rained without cease
all the time she was in Lausanne, and my eye
       sees her naked and gleaming with oils
       I've anointed her with. Because
I'm a man. And thoughts like these are my industry.

In an old engraving over her shoulder
        Victoria opens the Great
        Exhibition. Where to look now?
Her cigarette? The glow, the after, the ash?
        Her lips as she purses the smoke in?
        The drifting smoke as she exhales,
bodying forth the shiftless shapes of things to come?

It isn't wisdom, to be blind to beauty.
        She's on to Bratislava now,
        a figure-skating tournament,
Maria Butyrskaya, journalist friends.
        I think I need an oxygen tent.
        A transfusion of her. A bed
in intensive care. I'm sitting up once again

for the sake of a girl: this is work I love,
        and I'll try to number my days
        to apply my heart to wisdom –
for, whatever my industry, my desire,
        I also believe that *what we find*
        affectionate and rational,
that we may safely pronounce to be right and good.

New York, New York

The city knows us better, Kathrin, than we know ourselves:
the Hudson River, the street ravines, the subway, and the very light,
even the mounds of dirty snow and the uncollected garbage bags,
they all agree that three thousand miles apart is no place to be.

A city of water without the placable satisfactions of water.
A city of Gallic liberty without the sanity to be free.
A city of mock-European quirks on a dull Adelaidean grid.
A city of two great absences, and an overtowering presence.

Busy-bodied, querulous, unremitting,
Becky, the elder, bickers her sister to itsy-bitsy pieces,
a pitiless chicken obsessively pecking away,
stabbing its dinning beak over and over into an empty tin.

"Fuck you." And then "I love you, sis." And then "Fuck you" again.
It's like a souvenir ashtray falling and shattering into shards.
Who'll fit the pieces together again? And when? This is archaeology:
even from these remains I could write the eighteen-volume history.

Here on the Upper West Side, the city's a buried half-hearted effort.
The father, a mild-mannered spectacled shrike, picks off the shelf
another book of third-rate verse, pleasantly proselytising.
Who are these people? What is this city? Whose words are these
                                             on the page?

– Kathrin, my kisses return to your sex.
Across the wastes I have come, an animal to a salt-lick,
the past a privation, a purposelessness,
before me a freshness, a wetness, a tang.

WALK. I walk. DON'T WALK. I walk. The empire, still at peace,
goes about its business, undistinguished, savvy, occupied,
witless in its ironies: Osama bin Laden, in battledress,
on the *New Yorker* cover, studies the map of the subway.

In a Madison Avenue bistro I sit reading Aharon Shabtai.
"They've taken the word *peace* by the hair," he writes of his
                                                country's leaders,
"dragged it out of its humble bed, and turned it into their whore."
The empire, still at a peace of sorts, goes about business it understands.

Eliot, spirited, greyer now, of good cheer and resource,
walks me around his Village patch. His whole life is an essay.
He is a man who would notice the fall of a sparrow.
The empire, still at the kind of peace it understands, does business.

– That morning you were woken, Kathrin,
by hundreds of migrant geese in the neighbouring field,
did you not hear them repeating, as they rested on the flight,
that word of yours I've come to love, "somewhen"?

February 2003

94

Kiss / Bliss

What is it that psychiatrists tell you to do,
"Go to the happy place"? So I went to the happy place.
Jessica Lynch

We're in love but the terrified girl has a problem
the jittery private from Palestine

who as a child would hide in the refrigerator box
or anywhere on earth but in a convoy

near to Nasiriyeh shit we're off the road I'm telling you
this isn't the road and we kiss and they're hit

it's an ambush she's down on her knees as our mouths find the place
please don't let them don't let them don't let them don't let them

poor little clueless supply clerk from Palestine West Virginia
her fingers are fumbling the rest are returning

the fire and your fingers are inside my shirt
please don't let them sweet Jesus and something is hurting

she's hurt and your hand's on my heart please don't let them
the others are dead please don't let them don't let them

and ours is another place and we know nothing of this
let others believe in the myth and the lies if they like we're in love
and we kiss

pity the nation that needs an enemy
pity the nation that needs a hero

95

pity the terrified private whose problem
is bigger than any she faced at Fort Bliss

for she's broken an arm and a thigh and her best friend is dead
and the doctor is no one she knows she's

alone
far from home

and they're coming to get her to save her to lay her out
under a flag with a story for comfort

AMERICA LOVES JESSICA LYNCH
or so say a million magnets on refrigerator doors

but a nation isn't a father a mother a sister or a brother
nor is a nation now nor has it ever been a lover

a nation cannot love the beauties of your face
a nation cannot love your tenderness and grace

God bless by all means c'est son métier America
God bless the hapless American blonde and grant her an
                                                    American peace

I like to think that God prefers to bless
all those who find the one true happy place

Golbach

A handsome old comforting house it was,
crotchety, solid, and wise,
a house that would keep you warm when the world was a storm,
a house such as Horace had wanted, with trees and a stream,

with crooked cross-timbers and off-kilter beams
and a door with a cap like a churchyard gate,
and a fireplace backed with a coat of arms
that glowed with *Honi soit* when the wood was ablaze

and a great farmhouse oven for thirty good loaves
where the whole village formerly baked all its bread
and a resident marten that lived in the attic
and made the occasional ruckus when peace-loving right-
                              minded folk were a-bed

and mice that would skitter
down Tom Kitten passages
under the floors and the walls
and deposit their delicate shit in the kitchen

and (heavens!) the bees, the wild bees, that arrived with a
                              deafening drone like a 747
and blackened the air as I looked on in wonder
to see them, the thousands, the infinite thousands, move into
                              their seasonal quarters,
a hole in the timbers of (praise be!) my neighbour's,

and the phlox that would tender its scent to the stars
while the bats made their skeltering love to the night,
and the aconite, darker than midnight, hooded
in serious dangerous heart-breaker blue,

and the mighty black poplar, the wuthery nut trees,
the cowslips and ferns and the stream beyond,
and across in the meadow the wittering goats
and the geese that would save (I imagined) my Rome –

a handsome old house it was, but never a home
till you sat on the terrace, and dangled your legs, and put
                                        back your smile for the sun,
and set your dear heart's watch
by the topsy-turvy tappety-tap of the nuthatch.

The Wind at Vinci

The magi of day left their gifts and departed,
  and for a little while I lay awake
  as your breathing beside me rose and fell
    and the wind across the vineyards
shrilled and then keened and then darkened into a moan.

And the wind was as old as my fears, and it said:
  a man who has not learnt to know his home
  in an hour such as this will lie alone
    for the rest of his mortal days.
I thought of my dying father, one August night

unseasonably cold, that last of his summers,
  lost for his words and wanting to tell us
  the weather was wintry, instead (poor man)
    declaring in confusion: *What*
a horrible night! – it's like Christmas! And I thought

of my mother, a teenager after a war,
  thrilling to Mozart where fountains played in
  a courtyard amid the rubble, knowing
    that this was the meaning of peace.
So quickly a future is over; so quickly

the home we imagined we'd live for is lost; so soon
  the words and the music are wind. I thought
  of Leonardo too, his boyhood spent
    in the olive light of the groves,
accepting in manhood commissions to image

the Baptist inward and radiant with knowledge,
   the Saviour calmly foreknowing it all
   as he breaks the bread in the company
      of the man who will betray him.
It may be nobody has a home in the world,

but that is the way of the little night music,
   that is the point of the wind in the hills.
   Love (so the wonderful man from Vinci
      said) *is the offspring of knowledge.*
You smiled in your sleep; and I... I knew I was home.

The Secret History

Procopius knew what it was to be close
        to the rabble that call the shots
in an empire – their glowering fury
for war, command, humiliation, torture;
        their rage for immortality;

their battening greed to see dispensable
        others prostrated, disposed of.
The woman who had been *the common bane*
of all mankind (he wrote), who'd fuck every man
        at a dinner, then every one

of the menials, had shocked by becoming
        the Empress of Byzantium.
Naked she lay in the theatre now,
where geese especially trained to the purpose
        picked barley from her vagina.

One enemy she had chained to a manger,
        eating and shitting where he stood,
an ass in all but the braying: within
a month or so he had lost his mind, and died.
        Another was falsely accused

of buggering boys: she had his penis off.
        And then her long-lost son came home,
imagining his mother would be pleased,
and from the day he set foot in the palace
        was never seen again... Empress,

killer, whore, *vanitas* from her jewelled head
      to her preciously slippered feet,
empurpled, imperious trash – so close
to God, and so very nearly a god, so
      very nearly greater than God.

Watching you now, my love, contemplative, awed
      in the church of San Vitale,
the alabaster light on your upturned
face and the greatness of beauty unfolding
      within you like sun in a rose,

I know that love is indifference to power.
      Your eye has found the lamb, caressed
by Moses elsewhere in the mosaic;
your heart has gone out to the tenderness of
      the man, and the animal's trust,

and the nature of art that would turn away
      from power to record the gesture.
For the Lamb is the home of love: and you
wouldn't change with an empress, no, not for all
      the purple in Byzantium.

The Garden

God the first garden made, and the first city Cain.
Cowley

This is the city. The city you know. The city you have always known.
The dark has been dispelled. At night the city's domed with
noxious light,
a patient smothering of his own free will beneath a toxic tent.
By day it's bedlam. Even the indolent lilies of the field
are toiling and spinning as if there were no tomorrow. This is the city.
They settled, built, pulled down, built, destroyed, and built again.
They loved and built, laughed and built, warred and died and
wept and built.
This is the city. The city you know. The city you have always known.

The freeway's a jitter of metal and glass: it traffics you in
past the bearpits and brothels, the megastores, the multiplexes,
fast-food outlets, garden centres, abattoirs, internment camps,
and after the studios where they made that brilliant series about
the Plague,
after the gate where the emperors spiked the heads of enemies
and traitors,
after the acres of tenements and the urban planning office,
you come at last to a square the tourist board has deemed "historic".
All roads would lead you here. To nowhere. Have a nice day, Yorick.

Napoleon, Goethe, Zog of Albania, Sartre, Madonna, and Robert
Mugabe,
they all laid their heads on the pillows of the Grand Imperial Hotel.
The ancient library perished in flames in a single incendiary night,
but a reconstructed building stands in its place, with double
the number of books.
One of the seven who carried out the atrocities known as the
Sudden Deaths
was a dentist with a practice here, a pillar of the community.
From a Peugeot parked in a bay outside the Bank of the Wise and
the Foolish Virgins
a laptop was stolen containing the data of all of the meek who'll
inherit the earth.

Over there, in a cottage so woeful and tiny it's locally known as
The Coffin,
the lame projectionist lives, who works at the picture palace on
the corner:
given the chance, he'll recite every line of *Bicycle Thieves* or *Amélie*,
and he'll show you the scenes of your life, and remind you that
you could do very much better.
There lives the clockmaker; there the priest; and there the master
builder;
and there lives the victim who's due to be slaughtered at the
scheduled sacrifice
(every race and creed and colour takes a turn). And there's the gate
by which the Messiah will enter the city (so the people say) on
Judgement Day.

The people remember the days of black and white TV, the days
                                    of the Mongol hordes,
the days before Big Brother and the days before *Big Brother*.
The word of the age is "protection". They are addicted to their fears.
There's CCTV on every block. Their proverbs tell us everything.
The other man's grass conceals a cache of weapons of mass destruction.
Fine words butter democracies. A miss is as good as friendly fire.
It's an ill wind, whichever way it blows. No news is bad news.
Too many cooks are on TV. A watched kettle boils.

Their talk is of anthrax, botulinum toxin, yellowcake uranium oxide.
K. below Esthwaite at evening watches the bats go flittering
                                    under the trees.
Their talk is of football, cheap flights, credit, liberation, civilian
                                    deaths.
K. watches vultures over the Ebro, riding the currents, taking the
                                    updraft.
They give each other play stations, names, diseases, a big hand,
                                    a piece of their mind.
They download faith, hope and charity, instructions for use,
                                    indulgences.
K. is delighted by James Stewart in an old movie, as Elwood P. Dowd,
accompanied by his invisible friend, a white rabbit named Harvey.

This is the garden. The garden you know. The garden you have
always known.
Oh, the people will say, so that was how you spent your day.
As if I really might have put my time to better use.
But I have been watching the rise and fall of her breast as she sleeps,
the stir of a feather by her lips, the flush in her cheek like the
flush in a peach.
She loves her creatures. She cultivates her garden. She has no empire.
See her before this madonna of Bellini's, a tear in her eye
to see the infant clasping his mother's thumb in his little fingers.

For she is not only beautiful in herself but the cause that beauty
is in others.
For she is philosophy drawn from examples.
For she surprises by a fine excess, and not by singularity.
For she is a circle whose centre is everywhere and whose
circumference is nowhere.
For she is everything that is the case.
For she is the fulfilling of the law.
For she too is in Arcadia.
For she is the empress of ice-cream.

V

To our Unborn Daughter

after Sophocles

Daughter, this is a world of wonders. Birdsong in
    an April dawn.
        Sunlight in an orchard by a river.
Cherry blossom. Summer rain. Leaf-smoke in October. Snowfall. And

    the fragrances of apples, roses, rosemary,
        mown grass, wet earth.
        The taste of tiny forest strawberries.
And one of the stranger wonders of all the world is human kind.

    Birds of the air, fish of the seas, horses, oxen,
        asses, goats – how
        their self-applauding "lord" has used them! He's
mapped shipping lanes on the oceans, drawn up agricultural plans,

    bred fellow-beings to slaughter, and slaughtered his
        fellow-beings.
        And then he's talked his sanctimonious stuff
about saving the earth. Forgive humanity its vanity!

    If there's atonement, and reparation, they lie
        in language; laws;
        in lucent water-terraces of green
made to reflect the heavens of Java; in the labour of love

that makes a vineyard, a city, the thought of God;
in the carvings
of nameless artists at Urnes and Chartres;
in the music of Beethoven, poems of Wordsworth and Rilke;

in the touch that was brought to the marble and wood
by the hand of
Michelangelo, of Riemenschneider;
in the love that was in the looking in the paintings of Vermeer.

These, though not ours to give, are yours to inherit.
Welcome, dear soul.
The radiance that lights your mother's face
is the same that you know from your home. Daughter, now come
to our door.

Biographical Note

MICHAEL HULSE grew up in England, the son of an English father from the Potteries and a German mother from near Trier in the Mosel valley. After studying at St. Andrews he lived for twenty-five years in Germany, working in universities, publishing and documentary television, before returning to England in 2002 to teach at the University of Warwick.

His poetry has won him firsts in the National Poetry Competition and the Bridport Poetry Prize (twice), and Eric Gregory and Cholmondeley Awards from the Society of Authors, and has taken him on reading tours of Canada and the US, Australia, New Zealand, India, and several European countries.

He has edited the literary quarterlies *Stand, Leviathan Quarterly* and (currently) *The Warwick Review*, co-edited the best-selling anthology *The New Poetry*, and in the Nineties was general editor of the Könemann literature classics series and of Arc international poets.

He has translated more than sixty books from the German, among them works by Goethe, Rilke, Jakob Wassermann, W. G. Sebald, and Nobel Prize winner Elfriede Jelinek. He is a permanent judge of the Günter Grass Foundation's biennial international literary award, the Albatross Prize.

Michael Hulse is married and lives in Stafford.

Recent titles in Arc Publications'
POETRY FROM THE UK / IRELAND,
include:

LIZ ALMOND
The Shut Drawer
Yelp!

JONATHAN ASSER
Outside The All Stars

DONALD ATKINSON
In Waterlight: Poems New, Selected & Revised

JOANNA BOULTER
*Twenty Four Preludes & Fugues on
Dmitri Shostakovich*

THOMAS A CLARK
The Path to the Sea

TONY CURTIS
What Darkness Covers
The Well in the Rain

JULIA DARLING
Sudden Collapses in Public Places
Apology for Absence

CHRIS EMERY
Radio Nostalgia

KATHERINE GALLAGHER
Circus-Apprentice

CHRISSIE GITTINS
Armature

MICHAEL HASLAM
The Music Laid Her Songs in Language
A Sinner Saved by Grace

BRIAN JOHNSTONE
The Book of Belongings

JOEL LANE
Trouble in the Heartland

TARIQ LATIF
The Punjabi Weddings

HERBERT LOMAS
The Vale of Todmorden

PETE MORGAN
August Light

MARY O'DONNALL
The Ark Builders

MICHAEL O'NEILL
Wheel

IAN POPLE
An Occasional Lean-to

PAUL STUBBS
The Icon Maker

SUBHADASSI
peeled

LORNA THORPE
A Ghost in My House

MICHELENE WANDOR
Musica Transalpina
Music of the Prophets

JACKIE WILLS
Fever Tree
Commandments